The Everyday Vegetaria Cookbook with 70 Low l _ _ _ _ _ Breakfast and Dessert Recipes Inspired by the Mediterranean Diet

MW00876218

by **Vesela Tabakova**

Text copyright(c)2016 Vesela Tabakova

Table Of Contents

Vegetarian Slow Cooker Meals – Healthy Dinner Ideas Inspired by the Mediterranean Diet

We live in an age when everybody is constantly on the move and putting a home-cooked meal on the table during a busy weeknight is incredibly challenging. But no matter how hectic your day is, it is important that you take a moment and enjoy a good, hearty meal. Because while there may be more than one right way to eat, there is one thing all nutritionists agree on – the more real, natural, unprocessed food you consume, the better.

My slow cooker is my dearest kitchen appliance. It is easy to use, it saves energy, and is also easy to clean after you use it. What is even better - slow cooking is less of an exact science than pressure cooking or baking. As long as you always add enough liquid to to prevent burning, you shouldn't fear "messing it up."

My crock pot is an essential tool that helps me save time in the kitchen so I can spend more quality time with my loved ones. While it may look and sound difficult to cook healthy food at home, after trying out some of my delicious vegetarian slow cooker meals, you will soon realize you can produce a nutritious family dinner in no time. All my Mediterranean diet inspired recipes are super easy to throw together in the slow cooker in the morning. You just have to fill it up, plug it in, and come home to one of these cozy, comforting Mediterranean dinners that will warm your soul and nourish your body!

Weeknight dinner ideas are hard to come by. For me, preparing delicious slow cooker meals is the easiest stress-free way of cooking healthy, yet amazingly tasty food for the family. My Mediterranean recipes use simple ingredients that you probably already have in your freezer, refrigerator, and pantry. They do not require complicated cooking techniques and are simply the best solution for fast-paced families who want tasty and healthy meals.

Slow Cooker Appetizers and Snacks

Spinach and Artichoke Dip

Serves 4

Ingredients:

1 can artichokes, drained and chopped

2 garlic cloves, crushed

1 cup water

1 tbsp lemon juice

3 cups chopped spinach

1 tbsp fresh dill

1/2 cup crumbled feta cheese

16 oz sour cream

1/3 cup Parmesan cheese

Directions:

Add all ingredients in a slow cooker. Cover and cook over low heat for 1 hour.

Blend in a food processor, let cool for at least 3 hours, and serve.

Slow Cooker Hot Bean Dip

Serves 4

Ingredients:

2 cans refried beans

1 tsp hot paprika

8 oz sour cream

8 oz softened cream cheese

2 cups Monterey jack

2 cups shredded cheddar cheese

Directions:

Add all ingredients in a slow cooker. Cover and cook on high for 2 hours.

Broccoli Dip

Serves 4

Ingredients:

4 cups steamed broccoli florets

1/2 small onion, finely cut

2 garlic cloves, crushed

1 cup chopped spinach

1 tbsp lemon juice

1 tbsp tahini

8 oz cream cheese

8 oz sour cream

1/3 cup Parmesan cheese

Directions:

Add all ingredients in a slow cooker. Cover and cook over low heat for 1 hour.

Let cool for at least 3 hours before serving.

Slow Cooker Onion Dip

Serves 4

Ingredients:

2 cups chopped onions

3 tbsp olive oil

1/2 tsp thyme

8 oz softened cream cheese

1/2 cup mayonnaise

Directions:

Place onions, thyme, olive oil and pinch of salt into a slow cooker. Stir to coat, cover, and cook on high for 6-7 hours, or until onions are well caramelized.

Drain any liquid off the onions and combine with remaining ingredients in a bowl. Season with salt and black pepper to taste.

Slow Cooker Salsa

Serves 4

Ingredients:

3 lbs roma tomatoes, chopped

3 red bell peppers, chopped

1 small onion, finely cut

2-3 garlic cloves, chopped

3 tbsp olive oil

1 tbsp paprika

1 cup fresh parsley leaves, finely cut

1/2 tsp salt

Directions:

Place the tomatoes, onion, garlic, peppers, olive oil and paprika into the slow cooker. Season with salt, stir to combine, cover, and cook on high for 2 hours, stirring a couple of times during cooking.

Set aside to cool and pour in a food processor. Add in the parsley, blend, and serve.

Delicious Slow Cooker Hummus

Serves 4

Ingredients:

2 cups dry chickpeas

water, as needed

1/2 lemon, juiced

1 garlic clove, chopped

2 tbsp tahini

3 tbsp olive oil

1 tsp paprika

1/2 tsp cumin

1/2 tsp salt

Directions:

In a slow cooker, place the chickpeas and cover with water. Soak overnight then drain and rinse. Cook on low for 8 hours. Drain and reserve a cup of the liquid.

In a food processor, place the chickpeas, tahini, lemon juice, garlic, salt, cumin and paprika. Pulse until smooth, adding some of the reserved liquid as needed to achieve the desired texture.

Creamy Slow Cooker Mushrooms

Serves 4

Ingredients:

2 lbs cremini or button mushrooms, cleaned

4-5 spring onions, finely cut

1 cup finely cut parsley

1 garlic clove, chopped

1/2 cup vegetable broth

1 tbsp tahini

1/2 cup heavy cream

1/2 cup grated Parmesan cheese

1/2 tsp cumin

1/2 tsp salt

Directions:

In a slow cooker, arrange mushrooms across bottom and sprinkle with onions, garlic and parsley.

In small bowl, mix tahini and vegetable broth; pour over mushrooms. Sprinkle with salt and cumin.

Cover and cook on low heat for 8 hours. About 30 minutes before the end of cook time stir in heavy cream and Parmesan cheese. Taste for seasoning and more salt if needed.

Delicious Honey Glazed Carrots

Serves 4

Ingredients:

1 bag baby carrots

3 tbsp olive oil

½ cup light brown sugar

1 tbsp honey

1/2 tsp cinnamon

1/2 tsp ground ginger

4 tbsp finely cut parsley, to serve

Directions:

Place carrots in a slow cooker and stir in all other ingredients except parsley.

Cook on low 4-6 hours or until carrots reach desired tenderness. Serve sprinkled with parsley.

Cinnamon and Sugar Peanuts

Serves 4

Ingredients:

12 oz unsalted, roasted peanuts

1 tbsp melted butter

3 tsp ground cinnamon

⅓ cup brown sugar

Directions:

Place the peanuts, cinnamon and sugar in a slow cooker. Drizzle with butter, stir and cook on low, uncovered, for 3 hours, stirring occasionally.

Spread the peanuts onto a cookie sheet or parchment paper until cool and dry.

Slow Cooker Roasted Chickpeas

Serves 4

Ingredients:

2 cups dry chickpeas

water, as needed

1/2 tsp garlic powder

1 tsp paprika

1 tsp cumin

1/2 tsp salt

Directions:

In a slow cooker, place the chickpeas and cover with water. Soak overnight then drain and rinse. Cook on low for 8 hours. Drain.

Place chickpeas in the slow cooker and add in all other ingredients. Stir to coat and cook, uncovered, on low for about 10 hours, stirring occasionally.

Slow Cooker Soups

Creamy Zucchini Soup

Serves 4

Ingredients:

1 onion, finely chopped

2 garlic cloves, crushed

4 cups vegetable broth

5 zucchinis, peeled, thinly sliced

1 big potato, chopped

1/4 cup fresh basil leaves

1 tsp sugar

½ cup yogurt, to serve

Parmesan cheese, to serve

Directions:

Heat oil in a skillet over medium heat and sauté the onion and garlic, stirring, for 2-3 minutes or until soft.

Add the onion mixture together with the vegetable broth, water, zucchinis, potato and a teaspoon of sugar to a slow cooker. Cook on low for 6 hours or on high for 3 1/2 to 4 hours.

Season with salt and pepper, to taste. If you don't have an immersion blender, you can transfer the soup to a blender (in batches) and puree until smooth. Serve with a dollop of yogurt and/or sprinkled with Parmesan cheese.

l cubed

ined

1 carrot, chopped

2 garlic cloves, chopped

4 cups vegetable broth

1 cups chopped kale

3 tbsp olive oil

1 bay leaf

salt and pepper, to taste

Parmesan cheese, to serve

Directions:

Heat oil in a skillet over medium heat and sauté the onion, carrot and garlic, stirring, for 2-3 minutes or until soft.

Combine all ingredients except the kale into the slow cooker. Season with salt and pepper to taste.

Cook on high for 4 hours or low for 6-7 hours. Add in kale about 30 minutes before soup is finished cooking. Serve sprinkled with Parmesan cheese.

Broccoli, Zucchini and Blue Cheese Soup

Serves 4-5

Ingredients:

2 leeks, white part only, sliced

1 head broccoli, coarsely chopped

2 zucchinis, chopped

1 potato, chopped

4 cups vegetable broth

3.5 oz blue cheese, crumbled

1/3 cup light cream

Directions:

Add the leeks, carrots, broccoli, potato and zucchinis to the slow cooker. Pour the vegetable broth over all of the ingredients. Cook on low for 6 hours or on high for 3 1/2 to 4 hours.

Transfer the soup to a blender, add the blue cheese, and blend in batches until smooth. Pour the soup back into the slow cooker, add cream, and stir to combine. Season with salt and pepper to taste and cook on low for 10 minutes more.

Beetroot and Carrot Soup

Serves 6

Ingredients:

4 beets, washed and peeled

2 carrots, peeled, chopped

2 potatoes, peeled, chopped

1 medium onion, chopped

3 cups vegetable broth

1 cup water

2 tbsp olive oil

4 tbsp yogurt, to serve

a bunch or spring onions, cut, to serve

Directions:

Peel and chop the beets. Heat the olive oil in a saucepan over medium high heat and sauté the onion and carrot until tender. Add the sauteed onions and garlic, beets, potatoes, broth and water to the slow cooker. Cook on low for 6 hours or on high for 3 1/2 to 4 hours.

Blend the soup in batches until smooth. Return it to the slow cooker, season with salt and pepper and cook on low for 30 minutes. Serve topped with yogurt and sprinkled with spring onions.

Vegetarian Borscht

Serves 4-5

Ingredients:

4 beets, peeled, quartered

1 carrot, peeled, chopped

1 parsnip, peeled, cut into chunks

1 leek, white part only, sliced

1 onion, chopped

1/3 cup lemon juice

½ tsp nutmeg

3 bay leaves

4 cups vegetable broth

1 cup sour cream, to serve

3-4 tbsp finely chopped dill, to serve

Directions:

Place the beets, carrot, parsnip, leek, onion, lemon juice, spices and bay leaves in a slow cooker. Add in vegetable broth. Cover and cook on high for 4 hours.

Blend in batches and season well with salt and pepper. Return to the slow cooker and cook on low for 15 minutes. Serve topped with sour cream and dill.

Curried Parsnip Soup

Serves 4-5

Ingredients:

1.5 lb parsnips, peeled, chopped

2 onions, chopped

1 garlic clove

4 cups water

3 tbsp olive oil

1 tbs curry powder

½ cup heavy cream

salt, to taste

black pepper, to taste

Directions:

Heat the olive oil and sauté the onion and garlic together with the curry powder in a skilled. Add to the slow cooker together with the parsnips, water, salt and pepper, to taste.

Cover and cook on high for 4 hours. Blend in batches until smooth, return soup to slow cooker and stir in the cream. Cook on low for 10 minutes.

Pumpkin and Bell Pepper Soup

Serves 4

Ingredients:

1 medium leek, chopped

3 cups pumpkin, peeled, deseeded, cut into small cubes

½ red pepper, chopped

1 can tomatoes, undrained

3 cups vegetable broth

½ tsp ground cumin

salt and black pepper, to taste

Directions:

Combine all ingredients in crock pot. Season with salt and pepper and cook on low for 6 hours. Blend in batches and cook 15 minutes more.

Celery Root Soup

Serves 4

Ingredients:

2 leeks (white and light green parts only), chopped

2 garlic cloves, crushed

1 large celery root, peeled and diced

2 potatoes, peeled and diced

4 cups vegetable broth

1 bay leaf

2 tbsp olive oil

salt and black pepper, to taste

Directions:

In a skillet, heat olive oil, then add the leeks and sauté about 3-4 minutes. Add in the garlic and sauté an additional 40 seconds.

In a slow cooker, add the sautéed leeks and garlic, celeriac, potatoes, broth, bay leaf, salt, and pepper. Cover and cook on low heat for 7-8 hours. Set aside to cool, remove the bay leaf, then process in a blender or with an immersion blender until smooth.

Moroccan Pumpkin Soup

Serves 6

Ingredients:

1 leek, white part only, thinly sliced

3 cloves garlic, finely chopped

2 carrots, peeled, coarsely chopped

2 lb pumpkin, peeled, deseeded, diced

1/3 cup chickpeas

4 cups vegetable broth

5 tbsp olive oil

juice of ½ lemon

½ tsp ground ginger

½ tsp ground cinnamon

½ tsp ground cumin

salt and pepper, to taste

1/2 cup chopped parsley, to serve

Directions:

Heat olive oil in a skillet and gently sauté leek and garlic until soft. Add in cinnamon, ginger and cumin and stir.

Add this mixture to the slow cooker together with carrots, pumpkin and chickpeas. Add vegetable broth and salt and pepper.

Cover and cook on low 6 hours. Blend in batches and return to slow cooker. Cook for 10 minutes more. Serve topped with parsley

d quinoa, rinsed well

2 leeks ɪɪa. ɪ lengthwise and sliced

1 onion, chopped

2 garlic cloves, chopped

1 tbsp olive oil

1 can of diced tomatoes, undrained

2 cups fresh spinach, chopped

3 cups vegetable broth

salt and pepper, to taste

Directions:

Heat a skillet over medium heat. Add olive oil and onion and sauté for 2 minutes. Add in leeks and cook for another 2-3 minutes, then add garlic and stir.

Add sautéed vegetables and all remaining ingredients except the spinach into the slow cooker. Season with salt and pepper to taste. Cook on high for 4 hours or low for 6-7 hours. Add spinach about 30 minutes before soup is finished cooking.

Quinoa, White Bean, and Kale Soup

Serves 5-6

Ingredients:

½ cup uncooked quinoa, rinsed well

1 small onion, chopped

1 can diced tomatoes, undrained

2 cans cannellini beans, undrained

3 cups chopped kale

2 garlic cloves, chopped

4 cups vegetable broth

1 tsp paprika

1 tsp dried mint

salt and pepper, to taste

Directions:

Combine all ingredients except the kale into the slow cooker. Season with salt and pepper to taste.

Cook on high for 4 hours or low for 6-7 hours. Add in kale about 30 minutes before soup is finished cooking.

Serves 5-6

Ingredients:

½ cup uncooked quinoa, rinsed well

1 small onion, chopped

1 potato, peeled and diced

1 carrot, diced

1 red bell pepper, chopped

2 tomatoes, chopped

1 zucchini, peeled and diced

4 cups water

1 tsp dried oregano

3-4 tbsp olive oil

salt and black pepper, to taste

2 tbsp fresh lemon juice, to serve

Directions:

Heat the oil in a skillet and gently sauté the onions and carrot for 2-3 minutes, stirring every now and then.

Add sautéed vegetables and all remaining ingredients except the spinach into the slow cooker. Season with salt and pepper to taste. Cook on high for 4 hours or low for 6-7 hours. Add spinach about 30 minutes before soup is finished cooking. Serve with lemon juice.

Broccoli and Potato Soup

Serves 4-5

Ingredients:

2 lb broccoli, cut into florets

2 potatoes, peeled and chopped

1 large onion, chopped

3 garlic cloves, crushed

4 cups water

1 tbsp olive oil

¼ tsp ground nutmeg

slat and pepper, to taste

Directions:

Heat oil in a skillet over medium-high heat. Add in onion and garlic and sauté, stirring, for 3 minutes or until soft.

Add broccoli, potatoes, sauteed onion and garlic into the slow cooker. Add water, salt, pepper and nutmeg.

Cook on high for 4 hours or low for 6-7 hours. Blend in batches before serving.

Creamy Potato Soup

Serves 4-5

Ingredients:

4 medium potatoes, peeled and cubed

2 carrots, chopped

1 zucchini, chopped

1 celery rib, chopped

4 cups water

3 tbsp olive oil

1 cup whole milk

½ tsp dried rosemary

salt, to taste

black pepper, to taste

a bunch of fresh parsley for garnish, finely cut

Directions:

In a skillet, heat the olive oil over medium heat and sauté the onion and carrots for 2-3 minutes.

Add sautéed veggies and all remaining ingredients into the slow cooker. Cook on high for 4 hours or low for 6-7 hours then blend soup in a blender until smooth. Add a cup of warm milk and blend some more. Serve warm, seasoned with black pepper and parsley sprinkled over each serving.

Leek, Rice and Potato Soup

Serves 4-5

Ingredients:

1/3 cup rice

4 cups of water

2-3 potatoes, diced

2-3 leeks halved lengthwise and sliced

4 cups vegetable broth

3 tbsp olive oil

lemon juice, to serve

Directions:

Heat a skillet on medium heat. Add olive oil and sauté leeks for 2-3 minutes, stirring. Add sauteed leeks and all other ingredients into slow cooker.

Cook on high for 4 hours or low for 6-7 hours. Serve with lemon juice to taste.

Carrot and Chickpea Soup

Serves 4-5

Ingredients:

3-4 large carrots, chopped

1 leek, chopped

1 can chickpeas, undrained

4 cups vegetable broth

½ cup orange juice

2 tbsp olive oil

½ tsp cumin

½ tsp ginger

4-5 tbsp yogurt, to serve

Directions:

Heat olive oil in a skillet over medium heat. Add in the leek and carrots and sauté until soft.

Add this mixture together with orange juice, broth, chickpeas and spices into the slow cooker. Season with salt and pepper.

Cook on high for 4 hours or low for 6-7 hours. Blend until smooth, return to slow cooker, and cook for 10 minutes more. Top with yogurt and serve.

Spicy Carrot Soup

Serves 6-7

Ingredients:

10 carrots, peeled and chopped

2 medium onions, chopped

4-5 cups water

5 tbsp olive oil

2 cloves garlic, minced

1 big red chili pepper, finely chopped

salt and pepper, to taste

½ cup heavy cream

½ bunch, fresh coriander, finely cut, to serve

Directions:

Heat olive oil in a skillet over medium heat and gently sauté the onions, carrots, garlic and chili pepper until tender.

Add sauteed vegetables and 4-5 cups of water into the slow cooker. Season with salt to taste and cook on high for 4 hours or on low for 7 hours.

Blend in batches until smooth. Return to the slow cooker and stir in the cream. Serve with coriander sprinkled over each serving.

Lentil, Barley and Mushroom Soup

;

nts:

2 medium leeks, trimmed, halved, sliced

10 white button mushrooms, sliced

3 garlic cloves, cut

2 bay leaves

2 cans tomatoes, chopped, undrained

3/4 cup red lentils

1/3 cup barley

5 cups water

1 tsp paprika

1 tsp savory

½ tsp cumin

Directions:

Combine all ingredients into slow cooker and season with salt and pepper to taste. Cover and cook on high for 4 hours or on low for 8 hours.

Mushroom Soup

Serves 4

Ingredients:

2 cups mushrooms, peeled and chopped

1 onion, chopped

2 cloves of garlic, crushed and chopped

1 tsp dried thyme

3 cups vegetable broth

salt and pepper, to taste

tbsp butter

Directions:

Melt butter in saucepan and add mushrooms. Saute lightly.

Place mushrooms, vegetable broth, onion garlic, thyme and salt and pepper into the slow cooker.

Cook on low for 6-10 hours or high for 2.5-3 hours. Blend, season and serve.

Mediterranean Chickpea Soup

Serves 5-6

Ingredients:

1 can chickpeas, drained

a bunch of spring onions, finely cut

2 cloves garlic, crushed

1 can tomatoes, diced

4 cups vegetable broth

1/2 medium cabbage, cored and cut into 8 wedges

3 tbsp olive oil

1 bay leaf

½ tsp rosemary

½ cup freshly grated Parmesan cheese

Directions:

In a skillet, gently sauté onion and garlic in olive oil. Add to the slow cooker together with broth, chickpeas, tomatoes, bay leaf and rosemary.

Cook on high setting for 4 hours. Nestle cabbage into the soup, cover and cook until it is tender, about 20 minutes on high. Serve sprinkled with Parmesan cheese.

French Vegetable Soup

Serves 4-5

Ingredients:

1 leek, thinly sliced

1 large zucchini, peeled and diced

1 cup green beans, halved

2 large potatoes, peeled and cut into large chunks

1 medium fennel bulb, trimmed, cored, and cut into large chunks

2 garlic cloves, cut

4 cups vegetable broth

black pepper, to taste

4 tbsp freshly grated Parmesan cheese

Directions:

Combine all ingredients in slow cooker. Season with salt and pepper to taste. Cook on low for 6-10 hours or high for 2.5-3 hours.

Serve warm sprinkled with Parmesan cheese.

Minted Pea Soup

Serves 4

Ingredients:

1 onion, finely chopped

1 carrot, chopped

2 garlic cloves, finely chopped

4 cups vegetable broth

1/3 cup mint leaves

2 lb green peas, frozen

3 tbsp olive oil

1/4 cup yogurt, to serve

small mint leaves, to serve

Directions:

Heat oil in a skillet over medium-high heat and sauté onion and garlic for 2-3 minutes or until soft.

Add to a slow cooker together with the vegetable broth, mint, carrot and peas. Season with salt to taste. Cover and cook on low for 6-10 hours or high for 2.5-3 hours.

Blend in batches, until smooth. Return soup to slow cooker and cook for 10 minutes on low. Serve topped with yogurt and mint leaves.

Brown Lentil Soup

Serves 8-9

Ingredients:

2 cups brown lentils

2 onions, chopped

5-6 cloves garlic, peeled

3 medium carrots, chopped

2-3 medium tomatoes, ripe

6 cups water

1 ½ tsp paprika

1 tsp summer savory

Directions:

Add all ingredients into slow cooker. Cover and cook on low for 8 hours or high for 4 hours. Season with salt to taste and serve.

Moroccan Lentil Soup

ts:

1 cup red lentils

1/2 cup canned chickpeas, drained

2 onions, chopped

2 cloves garlic, minced

1 cup canned tomatoes, chopped

1/2 cup canned white beans, drained

3 carrots, diced

3 celery ribs, diced

6 cups water

1 tsp ginger, grated

1 tsp ground cardamom

Directions:

Add all ingredients into slow cooker. Cover and cook on low for 8 hours or high for 4 hours.

Season with salt to taste and puree half the soup in a food processor or blender. Return the pureed soup to the slow cooker, stir and serve.

Curried Lentil Soup

Serves 5-6

Ingredients:

1 cup dried lentils

1 large onion, finely cut

1 celery rib, chopped

1 large carrot, chopped

3 garlic cloves, chopped

1 can tomatoes, undrained

3 cups vegetable broth

1 tbsp curry powder

1/2 tsp ground ginger

Directions:

Combine all ingredients in slow cooker.

Cover and cook on low for 5-6 hours.

Blend soup to desired consistency, adding additional hot water to thin, if desired.

Simple Black Bean Soup

1 cup ⌐ ⌐d black beans

5 cups vegetable broth

1 large onion, chopped

1 red pepper, chopped

1 tsp sweet paprika

1 tbsp dried mint

2 bay leaves

1 Serrano chili, finely chopped

1 tsp salt

4 tbsp fresh lime juice

1/2 cup chopped fresh cilantro

1 cup sour cream or yogurt, to serve

Directions:

Wash beans and soak them in enough water overnight.

In a slow cooker, combine the beans and all other ingredients except for the lime juice and cilantro. Cover and cook on low for 7-8 hours.

Add salt, lime juice and fresh cilantro.

Serve with a dollop of sour cream or yogurt.

Bean and Pasta Soup

Serves 6-7

Ingredients:

1 cup small pasta, cooked

1 cup canned white beans, rinsed and drained

2 medium carrots, cut

1 cup fresh spinach, torn

1 medium onion, chopped

1 celery rib, chopped

2 garlic cloves, crushed

3 cups water

1 cup canned tomatoes, diced and undrained

1 cup vegetable broth

½ tsp rosemary

½ tsp basil

salt and pepper, to taste

Directions:

Add all ingredients except pasta and spinach into slow cooker. Cover and cook on low for 6-7 hours or high for 4 hours.

Add spinach and pasta about 30 minutes before soup is finished cooking.

Heartwarming Split Pea Soup

Serves 5-6

Ingredients:

1 lb dried green split peas, rinsed and drained

2 potatoes, peeled and diced

1 small onion, chopped

1 celery rib, chopped

1 carrot, chopped

2 garlic cloves, chopped

1 bay leaf

1 tsp black pepper

1/2 tsp salt

6 cups water

Grated feta cheese, to serve

Directions:

Combine all ingredients in slow cooker.

Cover and cook on low for 5-6 hours.

Discard bay leaf. Blend soup to desired consistency, adding additional hot water to thin, if desired.

Sprinkle grated feta cheese on top and serve with garlic or herb bread.

Minestrone

Serves 4-5

Ingredients:

¼ cabbage, chopped

2 carrots, chopped

1 celery rib, thinly sliced

1 small onion, chopped

2 garlic cloves, chopped

4 cups vegetable broth

1 cup canned tomatoes, diced, undrained

1 cup fresh spinach, torn

black pepper and salt, to taste

Directions:

Add all ingredients except spinach into slow cooker. Cover and cook on low for 6-7 hours or high for 4 hours.

Add spinach about 30 minutes before soup is finished cooking.

...... onion, finely cut

2 carrots, chopped

1 zucchini, peeled and cubed

1 box frozen baby Lima beans, thawed

1 celery rib, thinly sliced

2 garlic cloves, chopped

4 cups vegetable broth

1 can tomatoes, diced, undrained

1 medium yellow summer squash, cubed

1 cup uncooked small pasta

3-4 tbsp pesto

black pepper and salt, to taste

Directions:

Add all ingredients except zucchini, summer squash and pasta into slow cooker. Cover and cook on low for 6 hours or high for 4 hours.

Stir in pasta, zucchini and yellow squash. Cover; cook 1 hour longer or until vegetables are tender. Top individual servings with pesto.

Crock Pot Tomato Basil Soup

Serves: 5-6

Ingredients:

4 cups chopped fresh tomatoes or 27 oz can tomatoes

1/3 cup rice

3 cups water

1 large onion, diced

4 garlic cloves, minced

3 tbsp olive oil

1 tsp salt

1 tbsp dried basil

1 tbsp paprika

1 tsp sugar

½ bunch fresh parsley, to serve

Directions:

In a skillet, sauté onion and garlic for 2-3 minutes. When onions have softened, add them together with all other ingredients to the crock pot.

Cook on low for 5-7 hours, or on high for 3 1/2. Blend with an immersion blender and serve topped with fresh parsley.

Cheesy Cauliflower Soup

Serves 4-5

Ingredients:

1 large onion, finely cut

1 medium head cauliflower, chopped

2-3 garlic cloves, minced

4 cups vegetable broth

1 cup whole cream

1 cup cheddar cheese, grated

salt, to taste

fresh ground black pepper, to taste

Directions:

Put cauliflower, onion, garlic and vegetable broth in crock pot. Cover and cook on low for 4-6 hours. Blend in a blender.

Return to crockpot and blend in cream and cheese. Season with salt and pepper and stir to mix.

Creamy Artichoke Soup

Serves 4

Ingredients:

1 can artichoke hearts, drained

3 potatoes, peeled and cut into ½-inch pieces

1 small onion, finely cut

2 cloves garlic, crushed

3 cups vegetable broth

2 tbsp lemon juice

1 cup heavy cream

black pepper, to taste

Directions:

Combine the potatoes, onion, artichoke hearts, broth, lemon juice and black pepper in the slow cooker.

Cover and cook on low for 8-10 hours or on high for 4-5 hours or until the potatoes are tender.

Blend the soup in batches and return it to the slow cooker.

Add the cream and continue to cook until heated 5-10 minutes more. Garnish with a swirl of cream or a sliver of artichoke.

Tomato Artichoke Soup

Serves 4

Ingredients:

1 can artichoke hearts, drained

1 can diced tomatoes, undrained

3 cups vegetable broth

1 small onion, chopped

2 cloves garlic, crushed

1 tbsp pesto

black pepper, to taste

Directions:

Combine all ingredients in the slow cooker.

Cover and cook on low for 8-10 hours or on high for 4-5 hours.

Blend the soup in batches and return it to the slow cooker. Season with salt and pepper to taste and serve.

Slow Cooker Stews, Roasts and Sides

Eggplant and Chickpea Stew

Serves: 4

Ingredients:

2-3 eggplants, peeled and diced

1 onion, chopped

2-3 garlic cloves, crushed

8 oz can chickpeas, drained

8 oz can tomatoes, undrained, diced

1 tbsp paprika

1/2 tsp cinnamon

1 tsp cumin

3 tbsp olive oil

salt and pepper, to taste

Directions:

Spray the slow cooker with non stick spray.

Heat olive oil in a large deep frying pan and sauté the onion and crushed garlic for 1-2 minutes, stirring. Add in paprika, cumin and cinnamon. Transfer to slow cooker.

Add in eggplant, tomatoes and chickpeas. Cover and cook on low for 6-7 hours or about 4 hours on high.

Eggplant and Tomato Crock Pot

Serves: 4

Ingredients:

2 eggplants, peeled and diced

1 large onion, chopped

2 carrots, chopped

1 celery rib, chopped

2-3 garlic cloves, crushed

1 can garbanzo beans, rinsed and drained

8 oz can tomatoes, undrained, diced

1 tbsp paprika

2 bay leaves

1 tsp dried basil

salt and pepper, to taste

Directions:

Spray the crock pot with non stick spray.

Combine all ingredients in crock pot.

Cover and cook on low for 6-7 hours or about 4 hours on high. Discard bay leaves before serving.

Slow Cooker Mediterranean Stew

Serves: 6

Ingredients:

1 butternut squash, peeled, seeded, and cubed

2 tomatoes, diced

2 carrots, chopped

1 onion, finely chopped

1 zucchini, peeled and diced

1 eggplant, peeled and diced

1 celery rib, chopped

1 cup green peas, frozen

1/3 cup raisins

1 can tomato sauce

1 tsp sugar

1 tbsp paprika

1/2 tsp cumin

1/2 tsp turmeric

1 tsp black pepper

1 tsp salt

1/2 cup parsley, finely cut, to serve

Directions:

In a slow cooker, combine butternut squash, eggplant, zucchini, peas, tomato sauce, onion, celery, tomatoes, carrot and raisins. Season with salt and black pepper, add paprika, sugar, cumin and turmeric, and stir to combine.

Cover and cook on low for 6-7 hours or 4 hours on high. Serve sprinkled with parsley.

Green Pea and Mushroom Stew

Serves: 4

Ingredients:

2 cups green peas (fresh or frozen)

5-6 large mushrooms, sliced

3-4 green onions, chopped

2 cloves garlic

1 cup vegetable broth

1 tbsp paprika

1/2 cup finely chopped dill

salt and black pepper, to taste

Directions:

Combine all ingredients in crock pot. Cover and cook on low for 5-6 hours.

Garden Vegetable Stew

Serves: 4

Ingredients:

1 large onion, chopped

1 large bell pepper

1 zucchini, peeled and diced

1 lb okra, stem ends trimmed

1 cup green peas (fresh or frozen)

3 tomatoes, diced

2 cloves garlic, crushed

2 cups vegetable broth

1 tbsp paprika

salt and black pepper, to taste

1/2 cup finely chopped parsley, to serve

Directions:

Combine all ingredients in crock pot. Cover and cook on low for 5-6 hours. Serve sprinkled with parsley.

Tomato Leek Stew

Serves: 5-6

Ingredients:

2 lbs leeks, cut into rings

1 cup vegetable broth

3 tbsp tomato paste

1 tbsp dried mint

salt, to taste

fresh ground pepper, to taste

Directions:

Combine all ingredients in crock pot. Cover and cook on low for 5-6 hours.

Potato and Leek Stew

Serves: 4

Ingredients:

12 oz potatoes, peeled and diced

5-6 leeks cut into thick rings

1 cup vegetable broth

1/2 cup finely cut parsley

1 tbsp paprika

salt and black pepper, to taste

Directions:

Combine all ingredients in slow cooker. Cover and cook on low for 4-5 hours. Sprinkle with finely chopped parsley and serve.

Rosemary-Garlic Mashed Potatoes

Serves: 4

Ingredients:

2 lbs potatoes, peeled and diced

1/2 small onion, finely cut

3 garlic cloves, crushed

3/4 cup vegetable broth

1/4 cup milk

1 tbsp butter

1 tbsp dried rosemary

salt and black pepper, to taste

Directions:

Place the potatoes in a slow cooker. Add garlic, broth, rosemary, and salt. Stir to combine.

Cover and cook on high for 4 hours or until potatoes are tender. Pour in milk and butter, season with salt and pepper to taste and mash with a potato masher.

Hearty Slow Cooker Baked Beans

Serves: 8-10

Ingredients:

12 oz dried white beans

1 medium onion, finely cut

1 red bell pepper, chopped

1 carrot, chopped

1 cup water

1 tbsp paprika

1/2 tsp black pepper

1 cup parsley, finely cut

1 cup mint, finely cut

1 tsp salt

Directions:

Wash the beans and soak them in water overnight. In the morning discard the water.

Combine all ingredients in slow cooker. Cover and cook on high setting for 4 hours, stirring occasionally.

White Bean and Tomato Stew

Serves: 8-10

Ingredients:

1 can white beans, drained

1 medium onion, finely cut

3 tomatoes, diced

4 cups vegetable broth

1 tbsp paprika

1 cup parsley, finely cut

1 tsp salt

Directions:

Combine all ingredients except tomatoes in slow cooker. Cover and cook on high setting for 4 hours, stirring occasionally.

Add the tomatoes; stir, and cook for an additional 30 minutes on low heat.

Potato Broccoli Stew

Serves: 4

Ingredients:

2 lbs potatoes, peeled and diced

1/2 small onion, finely cut

3 garlic cloves, crushed

2 cups broccoli florets

1 cup vegetable broth

1/4 cup milk

1 tbsp dried rosemary

salt and black pepper, to taste

Directions:

Place the potatoes in a slow cooker. Add garlic, broth, rosemary, and salt. Stir to combine.

Cover and cook on high for 4 hours or until potatoes are tender. Pour in milk and butter, season with salt and pepper to taste and mash with a potato masher.

Rice Stuffed Bell Peppers

Serves: 4-5

Ingredients:

8 bell peppers, cored and seeded

11/2 cups rice

2 onions, chopped

1 tomato, chopped

1/2 cup fresh parsley, chopped

2 cups warm water

3 tbsp olive oil

1 tbsp paprika

salt and pepper, to taste

Directions:

Heat the olive oil and sauté the onions for 2-3 minutes. Add in paprika, rice, diced tomato and season with salt and pepper. Add ½ cup of hot water and cook the rice, stirring, until the water is absorbed.

Stuff each pepper with rice mixture using a spoon. Every pepper should be ¾ full. Arrange the peppers in a slow cooker and top up with the remaining warm water.

Cover and cook for 5-6 hours on low setting.

Bell Peppers Stuffed with Beans

Serves: 5

Ingredients:

10 dried red bell peppers

1 cup dried white beans

1 onion, finely cut

3 cloves garlic, chopped

2 tbsp flour

1 carrot, chopped

1 cup fresh parsley, finely cut

1/2 cup crushed walnuts

1 cup vegetable broth

1 tsp paprika

salt, to taste

Directions:

Put the dried peppers in warm water and leave them for 1 hour.

Cook the beans. Gently sauté onion and carrot and combine with the cooked beans. Add in the finely chopped parsley and walnuts. Stir.

Drain the peppers, then fill them with the bean mixture and arrange in a slow cooker, covering the openings with flour to seal them. Add vegetable broth.

Cover and cook on low setting for 4-5 hours.

White Bean Cassoulet

2 cans white beans, drained

10-11 white button mushrooms, sliced

2 leeks, finely cut

1 parsnip, peeled and sliced

2 carrots, sliced

2 cups vegetable broth

2 tbsp olive oil

1 tsp paprika

1 tsp crushed rosemary

1 tsp salt

Directions:

Heat olive oil in a large deep frying pan and sauté the leeks, carrot, parsnip and mushrooms for 2-3 minutes, stirring.

Combine all ingredients in slow cooker. Cover and cook on low for 7-8 hours.

Stuffed Grapevine Leaves

Serves: 6

Ingredients:

1.5 oz grapevine leaves, canned

2 cups rice

2 onions, chopped

2-3 cloves garlic, chopped

1/2 cup of currants

1/2 cup fresh parsley, finely cut

1/2 cup fresh dill, finely cut

1 lemon, juice only

1 tsp dried mint

1 tsp salt

1/2 tsp black pepper

6 tbsp olive oil

Directions:

Heat 3 tablespoons of olive oil in a frying pan and sauté the onions and garlic until golden. Add the washed and drained rice, the currants, dill and parsley and sauté, stirring. Add in lemon juice, black pepper, dried mint and salt.

Place a grapevine leaf on a chopping board, with the stalk towards you and the vein side up. Place about 1 teaspoon of the filling in the center of the leaf and towards the bottom edge. Fold the bottom part of the leaf over the filling, then draw the sides in and towards the middle, rolling the leaf up.

The vine leaves should be well tucked in, forming a neat parcel.

The stuffing should feel compact and evenly distributed.

Arrange the stuffed vine leaves in a slow cooker, packing them tightly together. Pour in some water, to just below the level of the stuffed leaves.

Cover and cook on low setting for 5-6 hours. Serve warm or cold.

Stuffed Cabbage Leaves

Serves: 8

Ingredients:

20-30 pickled cabbage leaves

1 onion, finely cut

2 leeks, chopped

1 1/2 cup white rice

1/2 cup currants

1/2 cup almonds, blanched, peeled, and chopped

2 tsp paprika

1 tbsp dried mint

1/2 tsp black pepper

½ cup olive oil

Directions:

Sauté the onion and leeks in olive oil for about 2-3 minutes. Stir in paprika, black pepper and rice and continue sautéing until the rice is translucent. Remove from heat and add the currants, finely chopped almonds and the peppermint. Add salt only if the cabbage leaves are not too salty.

Place a cabbage leaf on a large plate with the thickest part closest to you. Spoon 1-2 teaspoons of the rice mixture and fold over each edge to create a tight sausage-like parcel. Place in the slow cooker, making two or three layers.

Cover with a few cabbage leaves and pour over some boiling water so that the water level remains lower than the top layer of cabbage leaves.

Cover and cook on low setting for 6-8 hours.

Green Bean and Potato Stew

Serves: 5-6

Ingredients:

2 lbs green beans, rinsed and trimmed

2 onions, chopped

3-4 potatoes, peeled and diced

2 carrots, cut

4 cloves garlic, crushed

1 cup fresh parsley, chopped

1/2 cup fresh dill, finely chopped

1/2 cup water

2 tsp tomato paste

salt and pepper, to taste

Directions:

Place all ingredients except the potatoes in slow cooker. Stir to combine, cover and cook for 3 hours on low setting.

Add potatoes and cook for an additional hour. Serve sprinkled with fresh dill.

Cabbage and Rice Stew

Serves: 4

Ingredients:

4 cups cabbage, chopped

2 tomatoes, diced

1 cup long grain white rice

2 cups water

2 tbsp tomato paste

1 small onion, chopped

1 clove garlic, crushed

1 bay leave

1 tbsp paprika

1 tsp cumin

1/2 cup parsley, finely cut

salt and black pepper, to taste

Directions:

Combine all ingredients in crockpot. Cover and cook on low for 4-5 hours. Serve sprinkled with parsley.

Rice with Leeks and Olives

Serves: 4-6

Ingredients:

6 large leeks, cleaned and sliced into bite sized pieces (about 6-7 cups of sliced leeks)

1 large onion, cut

20 black olives pitted, chopped

2 cups hot water

1 cup rice

salt and black pepper, to taste

Directions:

Combine all ingredients in crock pot. Cover and cook on high setting 1 1/2 to 2 1/2 hours, stirring occasionally.

Rice and Tomato Stew

Serves: 6-7

Ingredients:

1 cup rice

1 big onion, chopped

2 cups canned tomatoes, diced or 5 big ripe tomatoes

1 cup water

1 tbsp paprika

1 tsp sugar

1 tsp savory

½ cup fresh parsley, finely cut

Directions:

Combine all ingredients in crock pot. Cover and cook on high setting 1 1/2 to 2 1/2 hours, stirring occasionally. When ready sprinkle with parsley and serve.

Vegetable Quinoa Pilaf

Serves 6

Ingredients:

1 cup quinoa

2 cups vegetable broth

1 red bell pepper, chopped

1 small eggplant, peeled and chopped

1 zucchini, peeled and chopped

2 spring onions, thinly sliced

2 garlic cloves, cut

1 tsp dried oregano

salt and pepper, to taste

1/2 cup shredded Parmesan cheese, to serve

Directions:

In a slow cooker, place quinoa and broth and top with remaining ingredients.

Cover and cook on high for 3-4 hours or on low for 5-6 hours. Fluff with a fork, top with Parmesan cheese and salt and pepper if desired. Serve immediately.

Slow Cooker Breakfasts and Desserts

is:

6 large apples, peeled and chopped

1/2 cup brown sugar

2 eggs

2 cups milk

a pinch of salt

1/2 cup quinoa, rinsed

1 cup steel cut oats

2 cups water

2 tbsp lemon juice

1 tbsp cinnamon

1/2 tsp vanilla extract

Directions:

Spray the slow cooker with non stick spray.

Layer the apples, brown sugar, salt, cinnamon, vanilla and lemon juice into the greased slow cooker. Do not stir.

In a bowl, whisk the eggs into the milk until smooth. Add the water and whisk again. Add in the oats and quinoa and stir to combine. Pour over the apple mixture.

Cook on low for 6-7 hours or on high for 3 hours.

Banana Bread Oatmeal

Serves: 4-5

Ingredients:

3 bananas, peeled and chopped

2 tbsp brown sugar

1 cup steel cut oats

2 tbsp chia seeds

2 tbsp ground flaxseed

3 tbsp raisins or chopped pitted dates

2 cups milk

2 cups water

1/2 tsp cinnamon

1/2 tsp vanilla extract

Directions:

Spray the slow cooker with non stick spray.

Place all ingredients in a slow cooker, stir, cover and cook on high for 3 hours, stirring occasionally.

Mediterranean Vegetable Omelette

Serves 5-6

Ingredients:

1 small onion, finely cut

1 green bell pepper, chopped

3 tomatoes, cubed

1 garlic clove, crushed

6-7 eggs, beaten

1/2 cup feta cheese, crumbled

4 tbsp milk

1/2 cup finely cut parsley

black pepper, to taste

salt, to taste

Directions:

Spray the slow cooker with non stick spray.

In a bowl, combine eggs, milk, feta, salt and pepper until mixed and well combined. Add onion, garlic, tomatoes, and pepper to the slow cooker and stir in the egg-cheese mixture.

Cover and cook on high for 2 hours. Start checking at 1 hour 30 minutes. Omelette is done when eggs are set. Sprinkle with parsley and serve.

Mediterranean Omelette with Fennel, Olives and Dill

Serves 5-6

Ingredients:

1 small onion, finely cut

2 cups thinly sliced fresh fennel bulb

2 tomatoes, cubed

1/4 cup green olives, pitted and chopped

6-7 eggs, beaten

1/2 cup feta cheese, crumbled

3 tbsp milk

3 tbsp finely cut dill

black pepper, to taste

salt, to taste

Directions:

Spray the slow cooker with non stick spray.

In a bowl, combine eggs, milk, feta, dill, salt and pepper until mixed and well combined.

Add onion, tomatoes, fennel and olives to the slow cooker and stir in the egg-cheese mixture.

Cover and cook on high for 2 hours. Check at 1 hour 30 minutes if the eggs are set.

Slow Cooker Omelette with Spinach, Roasted Pepper and Feta

Serves 5-6

Ingredients:

2-3 green onions, finely chopped

5 oz baby spinach

3 roasted red peppers, diced

8 eggs, beaten

1/2 cup feta cheese, crumbled

3 tbsp milk

1 tbsp finely cut dill

black pepper, to taste

salt, to taste

Directions:

In a skillet, sauté the spinach in olive oil for 2-3 minutes or until it wilts.

Spray the slow cooker with non stick spray.

In a bowl, combine the eggs, milk, feta, dill, salt and pepper until mixed and well combined.

Add the spinach, green onions and roasted pepper to the slow cooker and stir in the egg-cheese mixture.

Cover and cook on high for 2-3 hours. Check at 2 hours if the eggs are set.

Slow Cooker Cinnamon Apples

Serves 4

Ingredients:

8 medium sized apples, peeled, cut into eighths

1/3 cup walnuts, chopped

3/4 cup brown sugar

3 tbsp maple syrup

3 tbsp raisins

4-5 dried apricots, chopped

2 tsp cinnamon

2 oz melted butter

2 tbsp lemon juice

3 tbsp water

Directions:

Spray the slow cooker with non stick spray.

In slow cooker, toss apples and lemon juice to coat. Add in brown sugar, walnuts, maple syrup, raisins, apricots, melted butter and cinnamon. Stir to combine.

Cover and cook on low for 4-5 hours.

Slow Cooker Rice Pudding

Serves 4

Ingredients:

1/2 cup short-grain white rice

6 tbsp sugar

1-1/4 cups 2% milk

2 eggs, lightly beaten

1 cinnamon stick

1 strip lemon zest

pistachios, to serve

Directions:

In a slow cooker, combine the first six ingredients. Cover and cook on low for 2 hours.

Stir, cover and cook 1-2 hours longer or until rice is tender. When ready discard cinnamon stick and lemon zest. Serve sprinkled with pistachios.

FREE BONUS RECIPES: Vegetarian Superfood Salad Recipes for Easy Weight Loss and Detox

Kiwi, Strawberry and Mixed Greens Salad

Serves 4

Ingredients:

2 kiwis, cubed

6-7 medium strawberries, halved

2 cups mixed greens

1/2 cup croûtons

for the dressing

1/2 cup orange juice

4 tbsp olive oil

1 tbsp balsamic vinegar

1/2 tsp salt

Directions:

Prepare the dressing by whisking together orange juice, olive oil, balsamic vinegar and salt.

Cut the strawberries and kiwis. Arrange the mixed greens in a salad bowl and toss in the dressing. Add strawberries and kiwis on top and serve sprinkled with croûtons.

Warm Quinoa Salad

Serves 6

Ingredients:

1 cup quinoa

2 cups water

1/2 cup green beans, frozen

1/2 cup sweet corn, frozen

1/2 cup carrots, diced

1/2 cup black olives, pitted

2 garlic cloves, crushed

2 tbsp soy sauce

2 tbsp fresh dill, finely cut

3 tbsp lemon juice

2 tbsp olive oil

Directions:

Wash quinoa with lots of water. Strain it and cook it according to package directions. When ready set aside in a large salad bowl.

Stew green beans, sweet corn and carrots in a little olive oil until tender. Add to quinoa. I

n a smaller bowl, combine soy sauce, lemon juice, dill and garlic and pour over the warm salad. Add salt and pepper to taste and serve.

Quinoa and Black Bean Salad

Serves 6

Ingredients:

1 cup quinoa

1 cup black beans, cooked, rinsed and drained

1/2 cup sweet corn, cooked

1 red bell pepper, deseeded and chopped

4 spring onions, chopped

1 garlic clove, crushed

1 tbsp dry mint

2 tbsp lemon juice

1/2 tsp salt

1 tbsp apple cider vinegar

4 tbsp cup olive oil

Directions:

Rinse quinoa in a fine sieve under cold running water until water runs clear. Put quinoa in a pot with two cups of water.

Bring to a boil, then reduce heat, cover and simmer for fifteen minutes or until water is absorbed and quinoa is tender. Fluff quinoa with a fork and set aside to cool.

Put beans, corn, bell pepper, spring onions and garlic in a bowl and toss with vinegar and black pepper to taste. Add quinoa and toss well again.

In a separate bowl whisk together lemon juice, salt and olive oil and drizzle over salad. Toss well and serve.

Roasted Vegetable Quinoa Salad

Serves 6

Ingredients:

2 zucchinis, cut into bite sized pieces

1 eggplant cut into bite sized pieces

3 roasted red peppers, cut into bite sized pieces

4-5 small white mushrooms, whole

1 cup quinoa

1/2 cup olive oil

1 tbsp apple cider vinegar

1/2 tsp savory

salt and pepper to taste

7 oz feta, crumbled

Directions:

Toss the zucchinis, mushrooms and eggplant in half the olive oil, salt and pepper. Place onto a baking sheet in a single layer and bake in a preheated 350 F oven for 30 minutes flipping once.

Wash well, strain, and cook the quinoa following package directions.

Prepare the dressing from the remaining olive oil, apple cider vinegar, savory, salt and pepper.

In a big bowl combine quinoa, roasted zucchinis, eggplant mushrooms, roasted red peppers, and feta. Toss the dressing into the salad.

Quinoa with Oven Roasted Tomatoes and Pesto

Serves 6

Ingredients :

for the salad

1 cup dry quinoa

2 cups water

1 cup cherry tomatoes, for roasting

1/2 cup cherry tomatoes, fresh

1 avocado, cut into chunks

1/2 cup black olives, pitted

1 cup mozzarella cheese, cut into bite size pieces

for the pesto

1 clove garlic, chopped

1/2 tsp salt

1/2 cup walnuts, toasted

1 cup basil leaves

1 tbsp lemon juice

1 tbsp mustard

4-6 tbsp olive oil

1 tsp savory

2 tbsp water (optional)

Directions:

Preheat the oven to 350 F. Line a baking sheet with foil. Make sure the tomatoes are completely dry, then drizzle with olive oil and savory and toss to coat them all. Bake the tomatoes for about twenty minutes, flipping once, until they are brown. Sprinkle with salt.

Rinse quinoa very well in a fine sieve under running water; set aside to drain. Place two cups of water and quinoa in a large saucepan over medium-high heat. Bring to the boil then reduce heat to low. Simmer for fifteen minutes. Set aside, covered, for ten minutes and fluff with a fork.

Make the pesto by placing garlic, walnuts and 1/2 teaspoon salt in a food processor. Add basil, mustard and lemon juice and blend in batches until smooth. Add oil, one tablespoon at a time, processing in between, until the pesto is lightened and creamy. For an even lighter texture you can add two tablespoons of water. Taste for salt and add more if you like.

In a large mixing bowl, gently mix the quinoa with the tomatoes, avocado, olives and mozzarella pieces. Spoon in the pesto and toss to distribute it evenly.

Cucumber Quinoa Salad

Serves 6

Ingredients:

1 cup quinoa, rinsed

2 cups water

1 large cucumber, diced

1/2 cup black olives, pitted

2 tbsp lemon juice

2 tbsp olive oil

1 bunch fresh dill, finely cut

Directions:

Wash quinoa very well in a fine mesh strainer under running water and set aside to drain.

Place quinoa and two cups of cold water in a saucepan over high heat and bring to the boil. Reduce heat to low and simmer for fifteen minutes. Set aside, covered, for ten minutes, then transfer to a large bowl.

Add finely cut dill, cucumber and olives. Prepare a dressing from the lemon juice, olive oil, salt and pepper. Add it to the salad and toss to combine.

Fresh Vegetable Quinoa Salad

Serves 6

Ingredients:

1 cup quinoa

2 cups water

a bunch of fresh onions, chopped

2 green peppers, chopped

1/2 cup black olives, pitted and chopped

2 tomatoes, diced

1 cup raw sunflower seeds

3 tbsp olive oil

4 tbsp fresh lemon juice

1 tbsp dried mint

Directions:

Prepare the dressing by combining olive oil, lemon juice, and dried mint in a small bowl and mixing it well. Place the dressing in the refrigerator until ready to use.

Wash well and cook quinoa according to package directions. When it is ready leave it aside for ten minutes, then transfer it to a large bowl. Add the diced peppers, finely cut fresh onions, olives and diced tomatoes stirring until mixed well.

Stir the dressing (it will have separated by this point) and add it to the salad, tossing to evenly coat. Add salt and pepper to taste and sprinkle with sunflower seeds.

Warm Mushroom Quinoa Salad

Serves 4-5

Ingredients:

1 cup quinoa

2 cups vegetable broth

1 tbsp sunflower oil

2-3 spring onions, chopped

2 garlic cloves, chopped

10 white mushrooms, sliced

1-2 springs of fresh rosemary

1/2 cup dried tomatoes, chopped

2 tbsp olive oil

salt and freshly ground pepper

1/2 bunch fresh parsley

Directions:

Wash well the quinoa in plenty of cold water, strain it and put it in a saucepan. Add vegetable broth and bring to the boil. Lower heat and simmer for ten minutes until the broth is absorbed.

Heat oil in a frying pan and sauté onions for 2-3 minutes. Add garlic and sauté for another minute. Add sliced mushrooms and season with salt and pepper. Finally, add the rosemary. Stir fry the mushrooms until soft.

Mix well the cooked quinoa with the mushrooms and tomatoes. Serve sprinkled with fresh parsley.

Mediterranean Buckwheat Salad

Serves 4-5

Ingredients:

1 cup buckwheat groats

1 3/4 cups water

1 small red onion, finely chopped

1/2 cucumber, diced

1 cup cherry tomatoes, halved

1 yellow bell pepper, chopped

a bunch parsley, finely cut

1 preserved lemon, finely chopped

1 cup chickpeas, cooked or canned, drained

juice of half lemon

1 tsp dried basil

2 tbsp olive oil

salt and black pepper, to taste

Directions:

Heat a large, dry saucepan and toast the buckwheat for about three minutes. Boil the water and add it carefully to the buckwheat.

Cover, reduce heat and simmer until buckwheat is tender and all liquid is absorbed (5-7 minutes). Remove from heat, fluff with a fork and set aside to cool.

Mix the buckwheat with the chopped onion, bell pepper, cucumber, cherry tomatoes, parsley, preserved lemon and chickpeas in a salad bowl.

Whisk the lemon juice, olive oil and basil, season with salt and pepper to taste, then pour over the salad and stir. Serve at room temperature.

Spicy Buckwheat Vegetable Salad

Serves 4-5

Ingredients:

1 cup buckwheat groats

2 cups vegetable broth

2 tomatoes, diced

1/2 cup spring onions, chopped

1/2 cup parsley leaves, finely chopped

1/2 cup fresh mint leaves, very finely chopped

1/2 yellow bell pepper, chopped

1 cucumber, peeled and cut into 1/4-inch cubes

1/2 cup cooked or canned brown lentils, drained

1/4 cup freshly squeezed lemon juice

1 tsp hot pepper sauce

salt, to taste

Directions:

Heat a large, dry saucepan and toast the buckwheat for about three minutes. Boil the vegetable broth and add it carefully to the buckwheat.

Cover, reduce heat and simmer until buckwheat is tender and all liquid is absorbed (five-seven minutes). Remove from heat, fluff with a fork and set aside to cool.

Chop all vegetables and add them together with the lentils to the buckwheat. Mix the lemon juice and remaining ingredients well and drizzle over the buckwheat mixture. Stir well to distribute the dressing evenly.

Buckwheat Salad with Asparagus and Roasted Peppers

Serves 4-5

Ingredients:

1 cup buckwheat groats

1 3/4 cups vegetable broth

1/2 lb asparagus, trimmed and cut into 1 in pieces

4 roasted red bell peppers, diced

2-3 spring onions, finely chopped

2 garlic cloves, crushed

1 tbsp red wine vinegar

3 tbsp olive oil

salt and black pepper, to taste

1/2 cup fresh parsley leaves, finely cut

Directions:

Heat a large, dry saucepan and toast the buckwheat for about three minutes. Boil the vegetable broth and add it carefully to the buckwheat.

Cover, reduce heat and simmer until buckwheat is tender and all liquid is absorbed (five-seven minutes). Remove from heat, fluff with a fork and set aside to cool.

Rinse out the saucepan and then bring about an inch of water to a boil. Cook the asparagus in a steamer basket or colander, two to three minutes until tender.

Transfer the asparagus in a large bowl along with the roasted peppers. Add in the spring onions, garlic, red wine vinegar, salt, pepper and olive oil. Stir to combine.

Add the buckwheat to the vegetable mixture. Sprinkle with parsley and toss the salad gently. Serve at room temperature.

Roasted Broccoli Buckwheat Salad

Serves 4-5

Ingredients:

1 cup buckwheat groats

1 3/4 cups water

1 head of broccoli, cut into small pieces

1 lb asparagus, trimmed and cut into 1 in pieces

1/2 cup roasted cashews

1/2 cup basil leaves, minced

1/2 cup olive oil

2 garlic cloves, crushed

1 tsp salt

3 tbsp Parmesan cheese, grated, to serve

Directions:

Arrange vegetables on a baking sheet and drizzle with olive oil. Roast in a preheated to 350 F oven for about fifteen minutes or until tender.

Heat a large, dry saucepan and toast the buckwheat for about three minutes, or until it releases a nutty aroma. Boil the water and add it carefully to the buckwheat.

Cover, reduce heat and simmer until buckwheat is tender and all liquid is absorbed (five-seven minutes). Remove from heat, fluff with a fork and set aside to cool.

Prepare the dressing by blending basil leaves, olive oil, garlic, and salt.

Toss vegetables, buckwheat and dressing together in a salad bowl.

Add in cashews and serve sprinkled with Parmesan cheese.

Dried Fruit and Feta Cheese Buckwheat Salad

Serves 4

Ingredients:

1 cup buckwheat groats

1 3/4 cups water

1 celery rib, finely chopped

1 large endive, shredded

1/2 cup roasted walnuts, chopped

1/2 cup dried apricots, chopped

1/2 cup dried prunes, chopped

1/2 cup raisins

juice of half orange

1 tbsp balsamic vinegar

2 tbsp fresh mint, finely chopped

1/2 tsp salt

1/2 tsp black pepper

1 tbsp olive oil

3 oz feta cheese, crumbled

Directions:

Heat a large, dry saucepan and toast the buckwheat for about three minutes, or until it releases a nutty aroma. Boil the water and add it carefully to the buckwheat.

Cover, reduce heat and simmer until buckwheat is tender and all liquid is absorbed (five-seven minutes). Remove from heat, fluff with a fork and set aside to cool.

Combine dried fruit, buckwheat and all other ingredients in a large salad bowl. Toss to mix well and serve immediately.

Aluminum, Lentil and Rocket Salad

Serves 4

Ingredients:

1 cup brown lentils, cooked and drained

1 cup cherry tomatoes, halved

2 cucumbers, halved and thinly sliced

1/2 cup baby rocket leaves

1/2 red onion, finely cut

1 tbsp lemon juice

1 tsp honey

4 tbsp olive oil

6 oz haloumi, cut into slices

Directions:

Combine the lentils, tomatoes, cucumber, rocket leaves and onion in a salad bowl. Whisk together lemon juice, honey, olive oil, salt and pepper in a small bowl. Drizzle the dressing over the salad and toss to coat.

Pat the haloumi dry with a paper towel and toss in the remaining olive oil. Heat a frying pan over medium heat and cook the haloumi in batches, for one-two minutes each side or until golden. Transfer to a plate.

Divide the salad among serving plates. Top with haloumi and serve.

Brown Lentil Salad

Serves 4

Ingredients:

1 can lentils, drained and rinsed

1 red onion, thinly sliced

1 tomato, diced

1 red bell pepper, chopped

2 garlic cloves, crushed

2 tbsp lemon juice

1/3 cup parsley leaves

salt and pepper to taste

Directions:

Place lentils, red onion, tomato, bell pepper and lemon juice in a large bowl. Season with salt and black pepper to taste.

Toss to combine and sprinkle with parsley. Serve.

Baby Spinach Salad

Serves 4

Ingredients:

1 bag baby spinach, washed and dried

9 oz feta cheese, coarsely crumbled

1 red bell pepper, cut in slices

1 cup cherry tomatoes, cut in halves

1 red onion, finely chopped

1 cup black olives, pitted

1 tsp dried oregano

1 large garlic clove

3 tbsp red wine vinegar

4 tbsp olive oil

salt and freshly ground black pepper to taste

Directions:

Prepare the dressing by blending garlic and oregano with olive oil and vinegar in a food processor.

Place the spinach leaves in a large salad bowl and toss with the dressing.

Add the rest of the ingredients and give everything a toss again. Season to taste with black pepper and salt.

Tabbouleh

Serves 6

Ingredients:

1 cup raw bulgur

2 cups boiling water

a bunch of parsley, finely cut

2 tomatoes, chopped

3 tbsp olive oil

2 garlic cloves, minced

6-7 fresh onions, chopped

1 tbsp fresh mint leaves, chopped

juice of two lemons

salt and black pepper

Directions:

Bring water and salt to a boil, then pour over bulgur. Cover and set aside for fifteen minutes to steam. Drain excess water from bulgur and fluff with a fork. Leave to chill.

In a large bowl, mix together the parsley, tomatoes, olive oil, garlic, green onions and mint.

Stir in the chilled bulgur and season to taste with salt, pepper, and lemon juice.

Fatoush

Serves 6

Ingredients:

2 cups lettuce, washed, dried, and chopped

3 tomatoes, chopped

1 cucumber, peeled and chopped

1 green pepper, deseeded and chopped

1/2 cup radishes, sliced in half

1 small red onion, finely chopped

half a bunch of parsley, finely cut

2 tbsp finely chopped fresh mint

3 tbsp olive oil

4 tbsp lemon juice

salt and black pepper to taste

2 whole-wheat pita breads

Directions:

Toast the pita breads in a skillet until they are browned and crisp. Set aside. Place the lettuce, tomatoes, cucumbers, green pepper, radishes, onion, parsley and mint in a salad bowl.

Break up the toasted pita into bite-size pieces and add to the salad. Make the dressing by whisking together the olive oil with the lemon juice, a pinch of salt, and some black pepper.

Toss everything together until well coated with dressing and serve.

Greek Salad with Avocado

Serves 6

Ingredients:

2 cucumbers, diced

2 tomatoes, sliced

1 green lettuce, cut

2 red bell peppers, cut

1/2 cup olives, pitted

6 oz feta cheese, cubed

1 red onion, sliced

1 avocado, peeled and diced

2 tbsp olive oil

2 tbsp lemon juice

salt and ground black pepper

Directions:

Dice the cucumbers and slice the tomatoes. Tear the lettuce or cut it in thin strips. Deseed and cut the peppers in strips.

Dice the avocado. Mix all vegetables in a salad bowl. Add the olives and the feta cheese cut in cubes.

In a small cup mix the olive oil and the lemon juice with salt and pepper. Pour over the salad and stir again.

The Best Orzo Salad

Serves 6

Ingredients:

For the dressing:

1/3 cup extra-virgin olive oil

3/4 cup fresh lemon juice

1 tbsp dried mint

For the salad:

8 oz uncooked orzo

2 tbsp olive oil

a bunch of fresh onions, chopped

3 green peppers, diced

1/2 cup black olives, pitted, cut

2 tomatoes, diced

1 cup raw sunflower seeds

The dressing: Combine the olive oil, lemon juice, and mint in a small bowl, mixing well. Place the dressing in the refrigerator until ready to use.

Directions:

Cook the orzo according to package directions (in salted water) and rinse thoroughly with cold water when you strain it. Transfer to a large bowl and toss with the olive oil. Allow orzo to cool completely.

Once orzo is cooled, add the diced peppers, finely cut fresh onions, olives and diced tomatoes stirring until mixed well.

Stir the dressing (it will have separated by this point) and add it to the salad, tossing to evenly coat. Add salt and pepper to taste and sprinkle with sunflower seeds.

Blue Cheese Iceberg Salad

Serves 6

Ingredients:

1 small iceberg salad

1 avocado, cut

1 cucumber, cut

1 red onion, cut

1/2 cup walnuts, raw

5.5 oz blue cheese, coarsely crumbled

¼ cup orange juice

3 tbsp olive oil

1 tbsp honey

salt

Directions:

Tear the iceberg lettuce or cut it in thin strips. Toss it in a medium salad bowl together with the other vegetables.

Add the coarsely crumbled blue cheese. Whisk together honey, orange juice, olive oil and salt and drizzle over the salad. Toss in the walnuts and serve.

Apple, Walnut and Radicchio Salad

Serves 4

Ingredients:

2 radicchio, trimmed, finely shredded

2 apples, quartered and thinly sliced

4 spring onions, chopped

1/2 cup walnuts, roasted

1 tbsp mustard

1 tbsp lemon juice

1/3 cup olive oil

Directions:

Prepare the dressing by combining mustard, lemon juice and olive oil.

Place walnuts on an oven tray and roast in a preheated to 400 F oven for three-four minutes or until brown.

Mix radicchio, apples, onions and walnuts in a large salad bowl. Add the dressing and toss to combine.

Apple, Celery and Walnut Salad

Serves 4

Ingredients:

4 apples, quartered, cores removed, thinly sliced

1 celery rib, thinly sliced

1/2 cup walnuts, chopped

2 tbsp raisins

1 large red onion, thinly sliced

3 tbsp apple cider vinegar

2 tbsp sunflower oil

Directions:

Mix vinegar, oil, salt and pepper in a small bowl. Whisk until well combined.

Combine apples, celery, walnuts, raisins and onion in a bigger salad bowl. Drizzle with dressing and toss gently.

Greek Chickpea Salad

Serves 4

Ingredients:

1 cup canned chickpeas, drained and rinsed

1 spring onion, finely cut

1 small cucumber, deseeded and diced

2 green bell peppers, diced

2 tomatoes, diced

2 tsp chopped fresh parsley

1 tsp capers, drained and rinsed

juice of half lemon

2 tbsp olive oil

1 tbsp balsamic vinegar

salt and pepper, to taste

a pinch of dried oregano

Directions:

In a medium bowl toss together the chickpeas, spring onion, cucumber, bell pepper, tomato, parsley, capers and lemon juice.

In a smaller bowl stir together the remaining ingredients and pour over the chickpea salad.

Toss well to coat and allow to marinate, stirring occasionally, for at least 1 hour before serving.

Snow White Salad

Serves 4

Ingredients:

1 large or two small cucumbers -fresh or pickled

4 cups yogurt

1/2 cup of crushed walnuts

2-3 cloves garlic, crushed

1/2 bunch of dill

3 tbsp sunflower oil

salt, to taste

Directions:

Strain the yogurt in a piece of cheesecloth or a clean white dishtowel. You can suspend it over a bowl or the sink.

Peel and dice the cucumbers, place in a large bowl. Add the crushed walnuts and the crushed garlic, the oil and the finely chopped dill.

Scoop the drained yogurt into the bowl and stir well. Add salt to the taste, cover with cling film, and put in the fridge for at least an hour so the flavors can mix well.

Asian Coleslaw

Serves 4

Ingredients:

for the salad

1/2 Chinese cabbage, shredded

1 green bell pepper, sliced into thin strips

1 carrot, cut into thin strips

4 green onions, chopped

for the dressing

3 tbsp lemon juice

3 tbsp soy sauce

3 tbsp sweet chilly sauce

Directions:

Remove any damaged outer leaves and rinse cabbage. Holding cabbage from the base and starting at the opposite end shred leaves thinly.

Combine the vegetables in a salad bowl. Prepare the dressing by mixing lemon juice, soy sauce and sweet chilly sauce. Pour it over the salad and toss well.

Asian Carrot and Sprout Salad

Serves 4

Ingredients:

2 carrots, peeled and cut into ribbons

6 oz snow peas, trimmed, thinly sliced diagonally

2 cucumbers, cut into ribbons

1 cup bean sprouts, trimmed

1/2 cup snow pea sprouts, trimmed

1 tbsp sesame seeds, toasted

2 tbsp sunflower oil

2 tbsp rice wine vinegar

2 tsp sesame oil

1 tsp honey

Directions:

Mix sunflower oil, vinegar, sesame oil and honey and whisk to combine. Season with salt and pepper.

Put carrot and snow peas in boiling water and let stand for two minutes or until snow peas turn bright green. Drain, rinse under cold water and place in a salad bowl.

Add in cucumber, beans sprouts, snow pea sprouts and sesame seeds. Drizzle with dressing, toss to combine and serve.

Shredded Egg Salad

Serves 4

Ingredients:

3 large hard boiled eggs, shredded

2-3 spring onions, finely cut

2-3 garlic cloves, crushed

4 tbsp homemade mayonnaise

1 tbsp mustard

1 tbsp yogurt

1 salt and pepper, to taste

Directions:

Peel the shell off of the eggs. Shred the eggs in a medium salad bowl. Mix in the remaining ingredients. Serve chilled.

Fresh Greens Salad

Serves 8

Ingredients:

1 head red leaf lettuce, rinsed, dried and chopped

1 head green leaf lettuce, rinsed, dried, and chopped

1 head endive, rinsed, dried and chopped

1 cup frisee lettuce leaves, rinsed, dried, and chopped

3 leaves fresh basil, chopped

3-4 leaves fresh mint, chopped

4 tbsp olive oil

2 tbsp lemon juice

1 tbsp honey

salt, to taste

Directions:

Place the red and green leaf lettuce, frisee lettuce, endive, basil, and mint into a large salad bowl and toss lightly to combine.

Prepare the dressing from lemon juice, olive oil and honey and pour over the salad. Season with salt to taste.

Simple Broccoli Salad

Serves 4

Ingredients:

14 oz fresh broccoli, cut into florets

3-4 green onions, finely cut

1/3 cup raisins

1/3 cup sunflower seeds

1/2 cup yogurt

1/3 cup orange juice

1 tsp chia seeds

Directions:

Combine broccoli, onions, raisins, and sunflower seeds in a medium salad bowl.

In a smaller bowl, whisk together the yogurt, orange juice and chia seeds until blended. Pour over the broccoli mixture and toss to coat.

Caprese Salad

Serves 6

Ingredients:

4 tomatoes, sliced

5.5 oz mozzarella cheese, sliced

10 fresh basil leaves

3 tbsp olive oil

2 tbsp balsamic vinegar

salt to taste

Directions:

Slice the tomatoes and mozzarella, then layer the tomato slices, basil leaves and mozzarella slices on a plate.

Drizzle olive oil and balsamic vinegar over the salad and serve.

Bulgarian Green Salad

Serves 4

Ingredients:

1 green lettuce, washed and drained

1 cucumber, sliced

a bunch of radishes

a bunch of spring onions

juice of half lemon or 2 tbsp of white wine vinegar

3 tbsp olive oil

salt, to taste

Directions:

Cut the lettuce into thin strips. Slice the cucumber and the radishes as thinly as possible and chop the spring onions.

Mix all the salad ingredients in a large bowl, add the lemon juice and oil and season with salt to taste.

Green Superfood Salad

Serves 6

Ingredients:

4 cups mixed green salad leaves

2 cups broccoli or sunflower sprouts

1 avocado, cubed

2 cucumbers, chopped

1 tbs sunflower seeds

1 tbs pumpkin seeds

2 tbsp lemon juice

3 tbsp olive oil

1/2 tsp mustard

salt and pepper, to taste

Directions:

Mix all vegetables in a big salad bowl. Toss well to combine.

Prepare the dressing by whisking together olive oil, lemon juice and mustard. Season with salt and pepper to taste. Drizzle over the salad and toss again.

Sprinkle the salad with sunflower and pumpkin seeds and serve.

About the Author

Vesela lives in Bulgaria with her family of six (including the Jack Russell Terrier). Her passion is going green in everyday life and she loves to prepare homemade cosmetic and beauty products for all her family and friends.

Vesela has been publishing her cookbooks for over a year now. If you want to see other healthy family recipes that she has published, together with some natural beauty books, you can check out her Author Page on Amazon.

Made in the USA
Las Vegas, NV
09 October 2023

78848844R00073